is,

Country Music Library

Introducing
Country Music

ROBERT K. KRISHEF

Lerner Publications Company • Minneapolis

ACKNOWLEDGMENTS: The illustrations are reproduced through the courtesy of: pp. 4, 12, 19, 28, 36, 37, 41, 48, Country Music Foundation Library and Media Center; p. 9, Loudilla, Loretta, and Kay Johnson and the International Loretta Lynn Fan Club; p. 15, Independent Picture Service; pp. 23, 54 (left), 64, 71, RCA; p. 30, Jimmie Rodgers Memorial Foundation; p. 47, James R. Smith and Hank Williams, Jr. Enterprises; p. 54 (right), Heuck; p. 62, National Life and Accident Insurance Co., Nashville, Tennessee.

Front cover photos: Capitol Records (top left), RCA (bottom left), Heuck (right)

Back cover photo: Country Music Foundation Library and Media Center

LIBRARY OF CONGRESS CATALOGING IN PUBLICATION DATA

Krishef, Robert K.
Introducing country music.

(Country Music Library)
Includes index.
SUMMARY: A survey of the development of country music in the United States from its beginnings in colonial America and the rural South to its new popularity in the 1970s.

1. Country music—United States—History and criticism—Juvenile literature. [1. Country music—History and criticism] I. Title.

ML3930.A2K739   784   77-90148
ISBN 0-8225-1408-7

Manufactured in the United States of America. Published simultaneously in Canada by J. M. Dent & Sons (Canada) Ltd., Don Mills, Ontario.

International Standard Book Number: 0-8225-1408-7
Library of Congress Catalog Card Number: 77-90148

1 2 3 4 5 6 7 8 9 10 85 84 83 82 81 80 79

Contents

Arthur Smith and the Dixie Liners

Introduction

Imagine the following scene taking place sometime during the 1950s. An automobile driver in a large metropolitan area is stopped for a traffic light. While he waits for the light to change, he taps his fingers on the steering wheel in time to the music from his car radio. The music is loud enough to be heard by the people in the car that has just pulled up alongside. When the man realizes that, he quickly reaches over and starts punching buttons on the radio, as if looking for a good station. He has been listening to country music and doesn't want others to know, even if they are strangers he will probably never see again.

That scene wouldn't take place today, but 15 or 20 years ago city people felt that they were not supposed to like country music. Country music belonged in the poor, isolated rural areas it came from. Country performers, they thought, sang with a nasal twang, stomped their feet, talked with faulty grammar and strange accents, and made high-pitched, wailing sounds with their guitars.

The music wasn't cultured; it was undignified. Outsiders laughed at it, ridiculed it, sometimes got angry with it.

People even made public statements against country music. A Tennessee governor, Prentice Cooper, once said that Roy Acuff, then considered the "king of country music," was bringing disgrace to the state by helping to make Nashville the "hillbilly capital." A famous entertainment reviewer wrote that Johnny Cash couldn't hold a note and had "no vocal equipment." The president of a large corporation in Nashville remarked that Nashville was "a hard-working town, the country music image notwithstanding"; in his view, country music and hard work didn't seem to fit together.

Naturally, country performers and fans resented what they felt was the superiority complex of such "snob critics." The criticism and ridicule probably drove them closer together, much like family members loyally defending each other against outside attackers. The loyalty of country fans eventually became unique in show business. Rock stars have normally been only as "big" as their last hit records. But country singers have gone many years without a best seller and have still been able to draw crowds for their road shows throughout the country. And country performers have usually returned the loyalty of their fans. "The fans are my friends," was the way Loretta Lynn, the "queen of country music," once explained it; "if it weren't for them I would still be doing without."

Intense loyalty has also been a tradition among the members of the country music industry. For instance, Hank Williams, a legendary star of country music, never forgot the debt he owed to Fred Rose, a music publisher who had helped him early in his career. At one time Rose was trying to get a major recording contract for Hank, and a record company executive called the performer behind Rose's back. Williams angrily hung up at the suggestion that he sign a contract leaving Fred Rose out.

Country people have always been proud of the loyalty and the close personal feelings that hold them together. This pride and togetherness has no doubt contributed to the survival of country music in the face of the hostility directed against it. Yet country music has not just survived and has not remained only in the remote areas where it was born. It has spread through the nation and thrived even in the cities. The automobile driver in the large metropolitan area no longer has to be uncomfortable about others knowing that he's listening to country music. He has plenty of company among the other city drivers.

Probably half of the radio stations in the United States now play at least some country music. The television show "Hee Haw" is a top-rated syndicated program carried by more than 200 stations and seen by approximately 30 million viewers weekly. The American public spends about $2 billion annually on records and tapes; about one-fifth of that total is spent on country music. Country is second in popularity only to contemporary/pop music. It has come far since the days when it was a subject for ridicule.

Country music has succeeded nationally because it appeals to all people, regardless of how much money they make, what their occupations are, or where they live. It is true that the music originated predominantly with "poor folks" who knew what it was to chop cotton in the blazing sun or dig deep underground in coal mines. (A modern star, Bill Anderson, had a hit record entitled "Po' Folks," and he named his band the "Po' Boys.") But through the years, more and more people have realized that country music is talking to and about each of them. The typical themes—such as marriage problems, losing loved ones, loneliness away from home, and hope of life after death—are common to human experience. Almost everyone can identify with them and with the music.

A country song is actually a story or message set to music. The lyrics, not the melody, are most essential to the song's appeal. The singer's voices

Country music originated with poor people who sang about their troubled lives.

are not as important as their ability to tell a story with warmth and sincerity. In the words of Chet Atkins, country's strength lies in its "honesty," as compared to the "pretense" found in many Broadway songs. While there are those who would disagree with the reviewer who said that Johnny Cash had no vocal equipment, the important thing is that the reviewer missed the point of country music when he concentrated entirely on singing ability.

Since the message is the key to a country song, listeners must be able to hear, understand, and appreciate the lyrics. Therefore, the music must be comparatively simple. Often it is woven into a three- or four-chord structure and set three or four beats to the musical measure. True, there have been increasing exceptions in recent years. Some musicians and songwriters are turning to more complex rhythmic arrangements. The instrumental background can now include drums and a brass section as well as guitars and other stringed instruments. But the emphasis on the story has not changed.

Many of the stories themselves have not changed either. A newspaper columnist once complained that country artists had been singing the same songs for fifteen years. He was right about singing the same songs; but only in the sense that he would have been right, for example, about people poring over old picture albums or visiting places from their childhoods. He didn't understand the nostalgic influences that are basic to the country music tradition. Country fans are sentimental people whose emotions can be brought bubbling to the surface by a moving song, whether the song is old or new.

It is said that people "know a country song when they hear it." This is hardly a precise definition. The fact is, however, that there is no precise definition for country music. Country is a reflection, in good times and bad, of society and of the lives people live. It evolves as society changes. The Country Music Association once formed a committee to define country music, but the committee finally gave up. Now the rule of thumb most often used is something like that formulated by songwriter and performer Kris Kristofferson: "If it sounds like country, man, it is country."

Kristofferson wasn't referring to the surface sound, to singing with a rural twang. He was talking about the indefinable emotion that comes from within, the ability to communicate so honestly that the listeners feel a personal involvement with the song whether it is funny or sad. That involvement will be the basis for the country music of the future just as it was when country music began many years ago.

The Crook Brothers, 1932

Pre-1920s: Planting the Roots 1

It is impossible to say exactly when country music began. But there is little doubt that the rural entertainers who performed for the pleasure of their families and friends a hundred years ago were the musical ancestors of today's stars, of people like Johnny Cash Loretta Lynn, Merle Haggard, Waylon Jennings, Dolly Parton, and Glen Campbell. In searching for a beginning, one can go back even further—to the English, Scottish, and Irish settlers who brought their fiddles and their music with them to the new land.

These early colonists sang unwritten songs about kings and wandering minstrels, about sword fights and the sea, that had been handed down from generation to generation. The songs were called "folk songs" because they were stories set to music that were told and re-told by the "folk," the common people. Gradually these songs took on American characteristics. They became songs about the hazards of frontier life, about freedom, and about the railroad. They were influenced by the mingling of cultures—by British, French, Dutch, Negro, Mexican, and Indian people learning to live together. So the story-telling music began to fit the new American people. It ultimately led into the music that is now called "country."

Because country music has been the music of common Americans and has reflected the struggles of different kinds of people to make lives in a new nation, the Country Music Association has said that this kind of music "can rightfully claim the distinction of being America's only native art form." While some have disagreed with that opinion, all have agreed that country music did indeed grow up with the country.

Country music was not, however, found everywhere in the young United States. People of the cities were more "sophisticated" than their fellow citizens in remote, outlying areas. In the cities, the music was gentle, refined, classical. It was in the Appalachian Mountains, in the cotton fields, and in the small rural settlements, where Americans clung to the traditional, down-to-earth folk heritage, that folk music and later country music were made.

Country roots were strongest in the rural Southeast and South for several reasons. First, the people in these areas were isolated; therefore, they were less affected by the outside influences of a modern-

Many country music singers have been influenced by the music of black Americans.

izing society than were urban people. Their lives were hard—tragedy, exhaustion, and defeat were commonplace, and these have always been material for music "of the folk." The people in these areas were also extremely God-fearing; the danger of immoral behavior has been another theme common in country music. And finally, the people of the South and Southeast were in close contact with the blacks, whose own heritage was powerfully, mournfully, and spiritually expressed in song.

In fact, the influence blacks have had on country music shows just how closely the music is tied to the mingling of different peoples. Many white performers in the history of country music—singers like Jimmie Rodgers, Hank Williams, and Charlie Rich, and guitarists like Chet Atkins and Merle Travis—received their early training from blacks. Hank Williams was taught by an old street singer known as "Teetot." Williams had been thrilled at the way the elderly black man sang throbbing blues. But the tradition did not pass in a single direction from blacks to whites. Years later, in 1973, Charley Pride, a black musician, was named the Country Music Association "Entertainer of the Year." When he was asked how he had learned to sing country music, he answered, "Why, I learned by listening to Hank Williams."

Country music was, indeed, the music of all American peoples, deeply rooted in American history. It was sung at typically American gatherings during the latter half of the 19th century, when musical get-togethers were exciting events for country folks who often lived far from one another. They would gather for Saturday night house parties, or for special events such as barn raisings when all the people of the area would come together to put up a barn for one family and, of course, to celebrate. Some of these celebrations were called "barn dances." Years later many country music radio stations had programs of live music called barn dances. Even the famous "Grand Ole Opry," broadcast by WSM in Nashville, Tennessee, was originally called the WSM "Barn Dance," reminiscent of those early American rural celebrations.

The central attractions of those parties and dances were, of course, the best entertainers—the musicians, singers, square-dance callers, and humorous story tellers. They were not professionals; they were performing for fun, not for money. And they weren't considered stars, either—there wasn't a country music industry for them to be stars of yet.

But these celebrations prepared the way for the future industry and trained the musicians for stardom. The entertainers got experience and an informal taste of show business. The ones who were most skilled, who were most warmed and encouraged by applause, got jobs with the expanding circuit of minstrel shows and with the "medicine shows" (shows where medicines were sold that could, supposedly, clear up a wide variety of ailments).

Through the years country performers found more and more opportunities in entertainment. Fiddling contests were held with increasing frequency—and with increasing publicity—late in the 19th century. Winners of these contests were as popular with country folks as the heavyweight boxing champions John L. Sullivan and James J. Corbett were with the sports public. Not only fiddlers were recognized, though. Other musical instruments—the banjo and guitar—came along to add to or even replace the fiddle as the dominant instrument in frontier and rural areas. An aspiring musician could purchase a guitar for a few dollars from the mail order catalog of a new company, Sears Roebuck. People who could sing as well as play had more opportunity to show their versatility with the guitar than they did with the fiddle, so many musicians began using guitars.

By the early 1900s there was a sizeable group of recognized, talented musicians in the South and Southeast. Dr. Humphrey Bate of Nashville, a physician by profession and a harmonica player by hobby, had formed his own string band. Henry Whitter was well-known as a singer and guitarist around Fries, Virginia. Singer-banjoist Charlie Poole came out of western North Carolina. And two of the many accomplished fiddlers of the period were Eck Robertson, from Texas, and John Carson, from Georgia.

The performer destined to be the most famous of the early group of country musicians, however, was Uncle Dave Macon, a singer, banjoist, and humorist from Cannon County, Tennessee. Uncle Dave, whose nickname was the "Dixie Dewdrop," started like his contemporaries—by entertaining friends and neighbors at barn-raising celebrations, dances, and other community events. In 1918 a talent scout heard him at a party and signed him to appear for $35 at Loew's Theater in Birmingham, Alabama. Macon went on to become the first star of the "Grand Ole Opry." In 1966, 14 years after his death, he was named to the Country Music Hall of Fame.

Uncle Dave Macon was the first star of the "Grand Ole Opry."

Although there were many talented country performers as the 1920s approached, they were, professionally speaking, still stuck in their own areas. Macon and others were getting work on the "vaudeville circuit," the circuit of theaters presenting variety programs of song, dance, and comedy, but their bookings were limited to theaters in the South. For the most part, vaudeville promoters didn't think that the so-called "hillbillies" would succeed with the audiences of the urban North. Country entertainers may not have minded that, but they were probably frustrated by another obstacle, their inability to break into the record industry.

The record industry had existed since the 1890s, but it showed little interest in recording country artists. An exception took place in the early 1900s when the song "Arkansas Traveler" was cut on a wax cylinder (disc records were not yet in use) by Fiddlin' Bob Haines. This was probably the first country music recording ever made, but recording executives did not follow it quickly with others. They simply did not realize the potential market for songs by "hillbillies." It took another industry, radio, to begin the age of commercial country music.

The 1920s: An Industry is Born 2

Before the 1920s few people earned their livings solely from country music. They performed for pleasure and sometimes for a few extra dollars to supplement their regular jobs. Then two developments transformed country music into a commercial industry that performers could go into full time for money, not just for fun. First, many radio stations started programs featuring country artists. And second, record companies, convinced by the success of country radio, began releasing more country recordings.

Before 1920 there were no country music programs because there were no commercial radio stations. Then in 1920, radio stations began broadcasting in Pittsburgh and Detroit. After that, stations appeared so rapidly that, in about three years, there were more than 500 stations in the United States. Nearly 20 per cent of the stations were in the South, where people clung to traditional country music, partly because they were isolated. That same isolation made them appreciate radio, which linked them to the outside world.

But they did not want to hear from only the outside world on the radio; they also wanted to hear their own kind of music, music that was not available to them on records.

Radio stations were quite willing to give rural audiences what they wanted. In Atlanta, Georgia, WSB, founded in the spring of 1922, quickly put country artists on the air. It had some of the best-known talent in the area, talent like Fiddlin' John Carson and fiddler Gid Tanner and his Skillet Lickers, a group that included fiddler Clayton "Pappy" McMichen and Riley Puckett, a blind singer and guitarist. Another station, WBAP in Fort Worth, Texas, was probably the first to give the name "barn dance" to a program of country or hillbilly style dance music. Its barn dance began in 1923 and others followed.

One of the most successful barn dance programs of the era was launched in April 1924 by WLS Radio. WLS, although located in the Midwest (in Chicago), had a large audience in the South because of its strong signal. The WLS "Barn Dance" became the first nationally known program of its type. Bradley Kincaid, the "Kentucky Mountain Boy," was the star of the show in the late 1920s. Later, performers such as Gene Autry, Patsy Montana, and the comedians Homer and Jethro gained fame at WLS.

The chief announcer of the WLS "Barn Dance"

*Comedians Homer and Jethro gained fame on
the WLS radio program "Barn Dance."*

was a man named George Dewey Hay, known
as the "Solemn Old Judge." Hay was voted the
"most popular announcer in the United States" by
readers of *Radio Digest.* In the fall of 1925, he was
hired to manage WSM, a new station just opened
by Edwin Craig in Nashville, Tennessee. The
judge immediately decided to organize a WSM
"Barn Dance" similar to the program he had been
associated with at WLS.

The WSM "Barn Dance" went on the air in
November 1925. It was well received. Listeners
liked the music they heard from Uncle Jimmy

Thompson, Dr. Humphrey Bate and his Possum Hunters, Sam and Kirk McGee, the Crook Brothers, Uncle Ed Poplin and his Ole Timers, and others. The most popular star at WSM during those early days was Uncle Dave Macon, who joined the program in 1926. By 1927, the program was three hours long and was a Saturday night favorite for thousands of people.

Still, there was nothing to distinguish the WSM "Barn Dance" from similar barn dances on other stations—until Judge Hay made an ad-lib remark that became part of the history of country music. The "Barn Dance" was preceded by a program of classical music broadcast from New York City. This was the "Music Appreciation Hour," featuring music performed by the New York Symphony Orchestra. One Saturday evening after the symphony orchestra signed off, Hay said, "For the past hour, we have been listening to music taken largely from Grand Opera. But from now on we will present the "Grand Ole Opry." The name caught the attention of the public and gave the program a new image. Today WSM in Nashville still carries the "Grand Ole Opry," the program most closely identified with country music.

As the popularity of radio grew, the public's interest in records seemed to decline. Sales of radio sets, however, increased throughout the 1920s because of the greater number of radio stations with their entertaining programs, such as the "Opry" and the WLS "Barn Dance." Americans spent about $60 million for radios in 1922, and more than $842 million in 1929. During roughly the same period, the number of records purchased declined from about 100 million annually to less than 10 million. In the South especially, people were less interested in records. Obviously, they were getting their music over the radio.

Gradually record companies started giving opportunities to country artists. In June 1922, fiddlers Eck Robertson and Henry Gilliland were playing at a Confederate Veterans' Reunion in Richmond, Virginia. Impulsively, they decided to go to New York City after the reunion and try to break into the recording business.

They arrived a few days later, still wearing the western plainsmen clothing of their native states—Robertson was from Texas and Gilliland from Oklahoma. New Yorkers stared at them as they strolled down the street, fiddles in hand. When the two hillbillies walked unannounced into the office of the Victor Talking Machine Company, they caused amused surprise. Victor officials gave them a chance to audition, though. A few minutes later they had agreed to record the two fiddlers. The records produced that day were the first country releases on disc; Robertson's solo of "Sallie Gooden" is still considered one of the foremost examples of old-time fiddling.

After Robertson and Gilliland, other performers, like Henry Whitter, went to New York. More often, however, performers were discovered by talent scouts, who did much to develop the country music industry. The scouts took portable recording equipment with them and held auditions in many towns and cities. One scout, Frank Walker, recorded Charlie Poole and Gid Tanner and the Skillet Lickers; Arthur Satherly, another scout, discovered Gene Autry.

In 1923 Ralph Peer, a scout who was to help make the most significant early discoveries in the industry, was working for Okeh Records. An Okeh record dealer and wholesale distributor in Atlanta, Polk Brockman, suggested that the company record Fiddlin' John Carson, the popular fiddler with WSM Radio. The session took place in Atlanta in June of that year. Carson recorded "The Little Old Log Cabin in the Lane" and "The Old Hen Cackled and the Rooster's Going to Crow." Although Peer had been in the record business for about six years, this was his first exposure to country music. He frankly thought that Carson was terrible and never imagined there could be a market for such songs.

But Brockman was more optimistic. In fact, he was so sure the record would sell that he bought 500 copies immediately. Soon he placed an order for another shipment. Peer finally realized he had been wrong, so he listed the record in Okeh's catalog. For the first time a country release was nationally promoted and distributed. Carson's record is generally recognized as the beginning of the commercial country music industry.

Within about a year, numerous labels, including Columbia, Vocalion, Gennett, Brunswick, and Paramount, had joined Okeh in releasing country tunes. Among the few record companies to resist wholehearted participation was, oddly enough, the biggest—Victor. But Victor changed its mind after one of its singers, Vernon Dalhart, switched successfully from light classical and popular music to country.

Dalhart's real name was Marion Try Slaughter. He had many stage names in his career, which began in about 1916, but he was best known as "Vernon Dalhart." That name came from the two Texas towns between which he used to work as a cow puncher on cattle drives. By 1924 Dalhart's fortunes as a recording artist had waned. The Victor Talking Machine Company wasn't doing well either, so its executives accepted Dalhart's suggestion that he make a country record. The record Dalhart made, with "The Prisoner's Song" on one side and "The Wreck of the Old 97" on the other, quickly became Victor's best-selling release. Through the rest of the decade Dalhart had many

The original Carter Family

other country hits, including "The Death of Floyd Collins" and "Sydney Allen," and his total sales ran into the millions.

Convinced of the large market for hillbilly material, Victor hired Ralph Peer to find new country artists. Peer had already left Okeh Records and was operating his own publishing company. He agreed to work with Victor if his publishing company would get copyrights on the songs recorded and if he would receive royalties on record sales. Peer discovered many artists for Victor, but it was his recording trip to Bristol, Tennessee, in August 1927 that made him famous. If he had done nothing else, that trip alone would have secured his place in the country music industry.

On August 1, Peer recorded a group destined to become the "First Family of Country Music." This was the Carter Family — A.P., Maybelle, and Sara — whose style of gospel and folk music made a lasting impact on the industry. Then on August 4, Peer recorded a thin, sickly young man named Jimmie Rodgers, the "Singing Brakeman." Rodgers, country music's first superstar, recorded 111 songs in less than six years, before dying of tuberculosis in 1933 at the age of 35. He has been called the "Father of Country Music" because his short but enormously influential career helped lay the foundation for the growth of a young industry.

The "Father of Country Music," Jimmie Rodgers

The 1930s: A Golden Decade 3

Many people have been fascinated by the early history of commercial country music. John Edwards, an Australian who was killed in an automobile accident in 1960 when he was 28, was probably the most outstanding researcher and collector of early hillbilly records. Edwards studied the foundation-building era of country music enthusiastically. He believed that the period from about 1924 to 1941 was the "golden age" of country music. Many people have agreed with him, although the term "golden" seems an inappropriate description for the 1930s.

Late in 1929 the stock market crashed and investors lost an estimated $40 billion. During the following years, the United States suffered the worst depression in history. As many as 12 million people, 10 percent of the population, were out of work. More than 5,000 banks failed, and over 32,000 businesses went bankrupt. Obviously, the record industry and related industries were affected by the economy. Only six million records were sold in 1932. At the beginning of the 1920s, phonograph manufacturers were producing about two million instruments a year; early in the 1930s, they were making 40,000 a year.

Yet this was the time, according to John Edwards and others, when country music was enjoying its golden years. How could this be? Practically everything else was falling apart. Was country music immune to events happening all around it? The answer, of course, is no, although there were examples of immunity. In the bleakest moments of the depression, for instance, Jimmie Rodgers was proving the commercial appeal of country music. He was earning $100,000 a year, a remarkable sum for that period.

But Edwards was not measuring the golden age with a financial yardstick. He was considering the heart of the industry, not its pocketbook. Commercial country music was born in the 1920s, but during the 1930s it showed that it belonged. The fact that it could demonstrate its fitness in such hard times testified to its strength.

It was the loyalty of country folks to country music that solidified the industry. Sales of country records probably decreased somewhat during the depression, but most likely the percentage of decrease was far less than that of other types of music. Country fans, most of whom were poor even before the depression, nonetheless clung to their music. It was a beacon in their lives, keeping them from drifting off into discouragement. Many times when country people shopped at their local general stores, they automatically asked for the latest Jimmie Rodgers record along with their sacks of flour and coffee beans. The record cost 75 cents—a lot of money for those days—but people scraped together their precious pennies and supported country music.

More people began to make country music in the 1930s, too. Performers, or would-be performers, tried to be like Jimmie Rodgers, the Carter Family, and other stars. Some of the most famous country music careers—including those of Ernest Tubb, Bill Monroe, Bob Wills, Roy Acuff, Gene Autry, and Jimmie Davis—were nurtured during the golden decade of the 1930s. Davis, who went from show business to politics and served as governor of Louisiana twice, proved that country artists could be regarded seriously.

Although the record industry had fallen on difficult times, young artists could find opportunities on the rapidly expanding country radio shows, even though they sometimes had to work for nothing or for very little to get exposure. Many regions had important stations that helped young talent. Autry worked at KVOO in Tulsa, Oklahoma, for example, and Acuff started with WNOX in Knoxville, Tennessee. One group, the Carter Family, even played on a Mexican station, XERA, in the late 1930s. Stations like XERA, located just across the border, had such powerful signals that they could be heard throughout the United States.

Numerous stations had individual programs that contributed to their prestige. The oldest and best-known of them were the WLS "National Barn Dance" in Chicago and the WSM "Grand Ole Opry" in Nashville. But there were other highly successful programs featuring live entertainment, such as the WWVA "Jamboree" in Wheeling, West Virginia, and the WLW "Midwestern Hayride" in Cincinnati, Ohio.

Growing audiences made country radio appealing to sponsors. The Aladdin Mantle Lamp Company started advertising with the "National Barn Dance" in the early 1930s. In 1934 the "Grand Ole Opry" got its first sponsor, Crazy Water Crystals, manufacturers of an all-purpose medicine. Then national sponsors became interested in the country market. In 1935 a segment of the WLS "National Barn Dance" went on the National Broadcasting Company (NBC) network to advertise Alka-Seltzer, and in 1939 the R. J. Reynolds Tobacco Company bought a half hour of the "Grand Ole Opry" and put it on NBC.

Sometimes the performers themselves were ambitious enough to find sponsors. When Bob Wills and his band had trouble getting steady employment in show business, Wills convinced a local milling company to sponsor them at seven o'clock in the morning over KFJZ, Fort Worth, Texas. The company, Burrus Mill and Elevator, made Light Crust Flour, so the group became the Light Crust Doughboys. During the day the musicians drove trucks or did other work for Burrus, and at night they represented their sponsor in personal appearances.

A basic part of the country artists' success has long depended upon personal road appearances to establish a direct relationship between the performers and their fans. Early artists in commercial country music quickly realized that going on tour was an effective way of advancing their careers. By making themselves personally known in an area, they had a better chance of getting a radio job. And when they got a radio job, they usually got more money for their road shows.

In addition, the stations were promoted when their artists went on the road. By the mid-1930s both WLS and WSM had flourishing artists' bureaus that booked personal appearances for their talent. A mutually beneficial relationship developed, too, between the radio and record industries. At one time these industries had viewed each other as competitors; some stations had even refused to play records. But by the end of the 1930s, the radio and record industries had realized that each was

Tex Ritter was popular during the golden decade of singing cowboy films.

promoted by cooperating with the other.

In the 1930s country music gradually crept into new areas and found new fans, in part through the motion picture industry. The decade was the golden age of singing cowboy films. Gene Autry, Roy Rogers, and Tex Ritter were among the idols of the Saturday matinee crowd.

Cowboys were not new to the industry. Early popular singers like Goebel Reeves, Harry Mc-Clintock, Carl Sprague, Otto Gray, Jules Verne Allen, and Eck Robertson had their roots in the western territories. Western songs had the same simple touches and the same emphasis on lyrics as did other country music. In them, the locale of the themes was simply shifted from the mountains to the prairies.

Roy Rogers and the Cactus Cowboys

Country music was always changing and moving as the country grew. During the transitional decade of the 1930s, the industry, and the people in it, developed a sense of identity and a pride in themselves and in their music. They were ready for the dramatic changes that were to come in country music.

Minnie Pearl successfully combines humor and country music.

The 1940s: Out of the Hills

4

At various times traditionalists have wished that country music were the same as it used to be. In the 1940s such critics yearned for a return to the days when performers did not have a commercial profit motive, when country music was concentrated in regional pockets. Some felt that the golden age was destroyed by commercialism and expansion.

Others argued that there was nothing wrong with making money and that performers had a right to appeal to as wide an audience as possible. If one believed that country music should be maintained for the enjoyment of only a certain group, they asked, wasn't this reverse snobbery? Wasn't it almost like the attitude of those who had scoffed at the hillbillies?

The debate went on. But it didn't really matter whether or not the music was better or more sincere before the 1920s than it was in the 1940s. Nothing could have stopped the changes that had taken place. Since country had developed partly because of the isolation of its people, then obviously something different had to happen when the people were no longer isolated.

Radio began bringing the music out of the hills, breaking down the barriers of regionalism. Then during World War II, rural folks went to work in the factories and war plants of the cities and brought their music with them. Northern military personnel stationed in the South were deluged by the new musical sound. These population shifts made country music into a dramatic national phenomenon.

Early in the decade, the "Grand Ole Opry" organized a touring unit, called the Camel Caravan because it was sponsored by R. J. Reynolds, the company that made Camel cigarettes. The Camel Caravan's entertainers, such as Pee Wee King, Eddy Arnold, and Minnie Pearl, introduced country music and country humor to people at dozens of military bases and hospitals. In addition to sponsoring benefit performances, the "Opry" and other programs like the "National Barn Dance" and the "Renfro Valley Barn Dance" sent troupes out to perform for audiences who paid to hear them. Some of their shows drew as many as 10,000 fans.

The recognition of country music and performers was snowballing. Trade magazines like *Bill-*

Roy Acuff was one of America's most popular country singers during the 1940s.

board started carrying more articles and listings about hillbilly records and people in the early 1940s. By the middle 1940s the number of country radio stations had increased to more than 600. The show business accomplishments of artists like Roy Acuff were just as impressive as were the accomplishments of people in other branches of music. Acuff was earning hundreds of thousands of dollars a year. His recordings of "The Great Speckled Bird" and "Wabash Cannonball" sold in the millions. During World War II Japanese soldiers tried to anger Americans on the battlefield by shouting insults about well-known American personalities. Two of the people most often subjected to the Japanese insults, it is said, were Babe Ruth and Roy Acuff.

The financial success of country artists made them more resentful than ever of their negative hillbilly image. No one knows when or by whom the word "hillbilly" was first used, but it has been traced back to the *New York Journal* of April 23, 1900, which reported that "a Hill-Billie is a free and untrammelled white citizen of Alabama, who lives in the hills, has no means to speak of, dresses as he can, talks as he pleases, drinks whiskey when he gets it, and fires off his revolver as the fancy takes him."

That was hardly a complimentary description, although some country folks took it good naturedly. When Ralph Peer was recording Al Hopkins and his band in 1925, he asked Hopkins what to call the band. According to a researcher, Hopkins replied, "We're nothing but a bunch of hillbillies from North Carolina and Virginia. Call us anything." Peer laughed and named the band the "Hillbillies," which was the first time the word had been so officially used.

The choice was unfortunate, however, as far as most members of the young country industry were concerned. "Hillbilly" frequently became a word of ridicule. Bradley Kincaid and many other popular artists of the 1920s and 1930s hated it. By the 1940s calling a performer like Earnest Tubb a "hillbilly" to his face was like taking a physical risk. Tubb was among those who started to change the image. He persuaded his record company, Decca, to list him in promotion and catalogs as a "country" singer.

His ability to influence the company showed that artists were beginning to be regarded as individuals rather than as parts of a group, a radio program, or a show. When country music had been regional music, individuals were generally subordinate to their groups or to the programs they appeared on. But by the 1940s country music had stars who were respected in their own rights. Jimmie Rodgers started the trend. Roy Acuff followed. He was the first singing star of the "Grand Ole Opry" and was known as the "king of country music." With their individual influence, stars began to have some say about the industry.

In the 1940s industry innovators, among them Pee Wee King, Bob Wills, and Ernest Tubb, adopted electrical instruments. Tubb in particular felt that he needed the heavy, insistent beat of an electrical guitar. He often played in the rowdy night clubs, roadhouses, and taverns of the Southwest—the "honky-tonk" circuit, it was called—where an instrument had to put out a powerful sound to be heard.

Bob Wills started a new form of country music in the 1930s that swept over the nation in the fol-

lowing decade. His "western swing" was a blending
of jazz, Mexican music, old time fiddling, and big
band sound. Besides guitars and heavy-bowed
fiddles, Wills' music used saxaphones, drums, and
trumpets. What a difference this was from the traditional, down-to-earth country sound! An early
band had sometimes consisted of two musicians—
a fiddler and a guitarist, perhaps. Certainly it
seldom had more than four or five members. Wills'
bands were huge by comparison.

Yet country had always been the music of the
folks. Wills was clearly giving the people—many
of them, anyway—what they wanted. One of the
songs he wrote and recorded, "San Antonio Rose,"
became an industry classic. Other country singers,
as well as pop singers like Bing Crosby, recorded
it, too. Ultimately, an estimated eight million
copies of the song were sold.

Western swing and cowboy movies, along with
country radio and frequent personal shows in the
Southwest and West, helped the industry grow.
Because the West was important in country music,
the term "country and western" music came into
use. The term was better than "hillbilly" (anything
was), but it was not entirely accurate, nor was it
much appreciated by many in the profession.

"Western music" was a type of country music,
not a different kind of music. People with a traditional country heritage did not like "western"

being given more-or-less equal status with country music. On the other hand, some western performers felt they were being slighted by the country music establishment in Nashville. They were also annoyed to see country singers don fancy cowboy suits even though they had never been on a ranch in their lives.

All performers, no matter where they came from, were understandably sensitive to what was happening in Nashville. As country music spread to all regions of the land, the capital of the industry settled solidly in Nashville, the home of WSM's "Grand Ole Opry," by now the leading radio and stage show in the industry. In 1940 a movie was made about the program; in 1947 the Opry had a troupe perform at Carnegie Hall in New York City.

The Opry's main attractions, performers like Acuff, Tubb, Red Foley, and Eddy Arnold, were invariably among the most successful in the profession. On the Opry stage a star could be born seemingly overnight. Hank Williams, for instance, was nearly unknown when he made his debut there in 1949, but after singing "Lovesick Blues" and getting six encores, he was an instant hero.

In 1941 a squabble between the American Society of Composers, Authors, and Publishers (ASCAP) and the National Association of Broadcasters, an organization representing radio stations, speeded the development of both Nashville and the country music industry. ASCAP was a licensing body that collected royalties from radio stations playing the works of its members. When it wanted to charge stations a higher rate for rights to ASCAP music, the radio association refused to pay. This left stations with little music to play, since most composers, authors, and publishers were members of ASCAP. Then a small, competitive licensing organization, Broadcast Music Inc. (BMI), stepped into the breach. To get new compositions for radio, BMI signed up many country music people who had not been well represented, or not represented at all, by ASCAP. Country music benefited from the exposure. So did Nashville because many new country compositions were recorded there.

Gradually, other music businesses developed in Nashville to complement the performers and writers. In 1942 Roy Acuff and songwriter Fred Rose started the first country music publishing company. In 1945 Red Foley made a recording for Decca, the first record to be cut in Nashville. Shortly after, Ernest Tubb did a session for Decca. Then Steve Sholes of RCA Victor came to town with a country division; other record companies followed. Recording studios began to open in the mid-1940s, and record pressing plants, talent agencies, and other supporting businesses soon arrived.

By the end of the decade, Nashville's musical

activity was impressive. So were record sales and attendance at country music shows. It looked like the industry was headed for a new golden age in the 1950s, but the appearance was deceptive.

Hank Williams performed often at the "Grand Ole Opry."

Red Foley (left) *and Gene Autry* (center) *were both well-known performers on the "Ozark Jubilee" program.*

The 1950s: Surviving the Fall 5

At the beginning and the end of the 1950s, the country music industry was vigorous, and its executives and stars were optimistic. But the industry would just as soon forget the middle of the decade. As in the depression, country music had to survive a difficulty—in this instance, the sudden overwhelming popularity of rock and roll. Country music's survival proved again that its roots were strong, but the proof came hard.

Country performers enjoyed unprecedented national prestige as the new decade began. It wasn't uncommon for a performer to enter a bank after several months on the road and start pulling thousands of dollars out of his various pockets. A bank teller once asked Hank Williams how much he was depositing. "How do I know?" Williams replied. "My job is to make it. Yours is to count it."

The hillbilly image was not completely erased, though. When Jerry Lee Lewis received his first royalty payment for record sales, Sam Phillips of Sun Records gave him a check for $42,000. Lewis was suspicious, but Phillips assured him that the check was "as good as cash." So he took it to a hotel that cashed checks, and, of course, the hotel didn't happen to have $42,000 in its register. Lewis charged back to Phillips, convinced he had been tricked. Phillips finally had to arrange for Lewis to be paid in cash.

Incidents like these were understandable. Many performers had grown up in rural areas so different from the modern, urban world that they could not be expected to fit easily into city life. But it was also understandable—although it was unfair—for some big city folks to make sweeping, head-shaking judgments about the "hillbillies." The Nashville "blue bloods," members of the city's class-conscious upper society, resented the country entertainers with their flashy cowboy suits, their rough edges, their funny ways of talking, and, especially, their wealth.

Nonetheless, the image was gradually changing. Country music adapted itself to accommodate new stars of widely varying styles, from the traditional singing and guitar picking of Hank Snow to the clear, pure voices of Slim Whitman and Sonny James, who sang in the tradition of Vernon Dalhart.

Television, which became popular in the 1950s, was ideal for country performers, who had a flair for looking the audience (or the camera) square in the eye and singing with sincere warmth. Hank Williams made historic network appearances on the "Perry Como Show" in 1951 and on the "Kate Smith Show" in 1952. Portions of the "Grand Ole Opry" were shown on television and featured such artists as Ernest Tubb, Kitty Wells, Webb Pierce, Marty Robbins, Rod Brasfield, and Cowboy Copas. Many regions had syndicated local TV shows, like the "Midwestern Hayride," telecast out of Cincinnati, Ohio, the "Ozark Jubilee," from Springfield, Missouri, and the "Town Hall Party" (originally a radio barn dance show), from Los Angeles, California. Tex Ritter, Johnny Bond, and celebrated guitarist Merle Travis were among the nationally known performers who appeared on the "Town Hall Party."

Movies were still promoting country music. In the early 1950s, Ritter sang the hit theme song for the movie "High Noon," starring Gary Cooper and Grace Kelly (now Princess Grace of Monaco). Many city people left the theater humming the theme without realizing that the tune they liked so much was country.

Country music also showed its versatility in "crossover" record hits, best sellers on both the pop music charts and the country charts, which occurred with increasing frequency in the 1950s. "Chattanooga Shoe Shine Boy" was a million-plus seller for Red Foley. An especially famous crossover was "Tennessee Waltz," written by Pee Wee King and Redd Stewart, the vocalist with his band. This record had modest success as a country tune but really took off when recorded by pop singer Patti Page. In six months nearly five million copies were sold.

Hank Williams was the individual most responsible for the acceptance of country material into the pop music world. In 1951 a young singer named Tony Bennett catapulted to stardom with his recording of Williams's song "Cold, Cold Heart." After that Hank wrote many other hits that were recorded as crossovers. Among them were "Half as Much" by Rosemary Clooney, "Jambalaya" by Jo Stafford, and "Hey, Good Lookin'" by Frankie Laine. One of Williams's songs, "Your Cheating Heart," was recorded by more than 50 different artists.

A country artist himself even crossed over into the pop field in the 1950s. He was Eddy Arnold, a "crooning" singer who had had such hits as "Bouquet of Roses," "I Really Don't Want to Know," and "Make the World Go Away." Arnold, the son of a west Tennessee sharecropper and once known professionally as the "Tennessee Plowboy," left the Grand Ole Opry for an eventual network television career. Arnold also made concert appearances dressed in, of all things, a tuxedo, and serious music patrons paid $10 (a large sum then) to see him perform. Some die-hard country fans never forgave Arnold for deserting his country music heritage.

In a sense, the problems of the mid-1950s were caused by crossover artists. One of the most important of these was a country musician named Bill Haley, who had experienced only mediocre success early in the decade. At the same time, rock and roll was hovering on the fringes of a commercial breakthrough. Haley and his Comets accomplished the breakthrough for rock and roll in 1954 when they recorded "Rock around the Clock," which they also sang as the theme for the movie "The Blackboard Jungle."

Rock and roll quickly became country music's most difficult competition. But even it had a king with a country heritage. The king of the rock and roll revolution was, of course, Elvis Presley. Presley was born in Tupelo, Mississippi, and raised on a musical diet of gospel and country. He started as a country musician and performed on the "Louisiana Hayride" out of Shreveport, Louisiana. Musically he was influenced by his association with blacks, just as Jimmie Rodgers, Hank Williams, and many others were. But Presley cultivated his own style in which the rhythmic rock beat was far more important than the lyrics.

Rock music surged over the entertainment industry, devastating the competition. The number of radio stations playing country music dropped to a handful. Except for the "Grand Ole Opry," radio barn dance programs went out of business. Country record sales dropped drastically, and many country musicians found it almost impossible to get work. Some performers—those who were able to adapt, and who wished to—decided to join the opposition. Jerry Lee Lewis, Carl Perkins, and Conway Twitty were among the country musicians who became rock and roll stars in the 1950s.

But the country industry fought back. The formation of a disc jockey association in 1954 led two years later to the formation of the Country Music Association, which vigorously promoted the welfare of country music. New stars like Johnny Cash rose to prominence on the strength of powerful,

country-flavored lyrics about "walking the line" or "being stuck in Folsom Prison."

Near the end of the decade, the resurging interest in a branch of country music called "bluegrass" also helped to stabilize the industry. Bluegrass was folk or country music with "overdrive"—it was fast-paced. A bluegrass band was a string band that usually used guitar, bass, banjo, mandolin, and fiddle, with the banjo as the dominant solo instrument. The vocals and the instrumentals were high-pitched.

Historian Bill Malone called the bluegrass style the "direct descendant of the hillbilly string bands of the 1920s and 1930s." The name "bluegrass" became popular in the 1950s because of Bill Monroe, who came from the Blue Grass State of Kentucky and who called his band the "Blue Grass Boys." Considered the "Father of Bluegrass," Monroe started playing in the 1930s with his brothers, Charley and Birch. He formed his own group in 1938 and joined the "Grand Ole Opry" in 1939. Scores of modern bluegrass greats, including Earl Scruggs, Lester Flatt, Mac Wiseman, Don Reno, Jimmy Martin, Carter Stanley, and Sonny Osborne, learned from Monroe as members of his organization.

Several reasons have been advanced to explain the bluegrass revival. Traditional bluegrass bands did not use electrical instruments. Thus the music was as refreshingly different from the thundering rock and roll sound as rock had been from other music a few years earlier. College crowds in particular took to musicians such as Earl Scruggs, who was widely acclaimed for his artistry on the five-string banjo. Articles on bluegrass appeared in *Time* and *Esquire*. Alan Lomax, a leading folklorist, wrote that bluegrass was the "freshest sound" in American folk music.

Ironically, the fresh sound was really an old sound. Probably even before the 1920s, it had been bridging the gaps between eras of country music. Now it was helping to rebuild the country music industry in preparation for a new decade and another new sound.

The 1960s:
The Nashville Sound 6

Traditionalists had mixed feelings about what had happened to "their" music during the 1950s. They were happy that it had lived through the difficult times, of course, instead of fading out nationally and becoming only regional music again. Traditionalists were not, however, happy about the new country sounds that kept cropping up to plague them.

Yet some of the old sounds were stronger than ever, thanks to the stirring bluegrass revival. Audiences were ready again for examples of hard country—direct, story-telling songs presented with sincerity by people who knew what they were talking about. "When a hillbilly sings 'I Laid My Mother Away,'" Hank Williams once said, "he sees her in the coffin." Williams felt that hillbillies sang more sincerely than most entertainers because they came from rougher environments. "You got to know a lot about hard work," he said.

Several rural people who knew what hard life was became stars in the 1960s. They included George Jones, Loretta Lynn, Porter Wagoner, and Merle Haggard. Wagoner started, and still has, one of the most successful syndicated television shows in the entertainment business. Haggard, an ex-convict, sang and wrote from the heart about his depression childhood ("Mama Tried"), his ditch digging and other back-breaking work ("Workin' Man Blues"), and his years in prison ("Branded Man"). Haggard always remembered his prison experience. Once when he was talking to Johnny Cash, a reference was made to the album Cash had recorded live at San Quentin Prison. Haggard said, yes, he recalled. Cash was puzzled. "Why, I don't remember you being on that show, Merle." "I was in the audience, Johnny," Haggard responded quietly.

The revitalization of country music brought another result along with the return to old sounds. It made Nashville an entertainment center for music other than country. Some years earlier, David Cobb, a radio personality with WSM, had named the city "Music City, U.S.A." The name may have been promotional at first, but it was accurate by the '60s. Nashville had been recognized because one could hardly ignore a city that produced millions of dollars through records, song publishing, and other music-related industries. In the 1960s it was respected as well because of the professionalism of its facilities and the talent of its musicians.

All sorts of entertainers—Bob Dylan, Frank Sinatra, Dean Martin, Dinah Shore, Ann-Margaret, and many others—started coming to town to cut record albums. Recording sessions had an informality that fascinated performers from other backgrounds. New performers responded with near disbelief, like network radio executives had when they had seen the "Grand Ole Opry" for the first time.

The Opry radio and stage shows had always been loosely produced. There were no rehearsals; the stage swarmed with people; fans ran up to photograph their favorites. Yet the show worked, and one reason, Opry officials explained patiently to visitors, was the natural, spontaneous atmosphere.

At recording sessions, too, the "pickers" and sidemen had a loose, easy style that evolved from their musical upbringings. Most of them were self-taught. When a country musician from Nashville went to a session elsewhere and was asked if he could read music, he was fond of answering, "Not enough to hurt my picking, man." Through the years, Nashville musicians developed their own musical code, using numbers instead of musical notations. "It's amazing," said Broadway performer

Carol Channing. "They just write down these numbers, and then they play the song."

Gradually a title emerged for the sound at these sessions: the Nashville sound. It was hard to define, just as country music had been hard to define. "I've been asked what the Nashville sound is a thousand times," said music producer Owen Bradley, "and I've given a thousand answers." Chet Atkins, one of the greatest guitarists in the history of country music, believes that technically there is no such thing as the Nashville sound. "It's the relaxed mood of the musicians, an attitude, rather than an engineering or musical approach," he said.

However, Atkins, who later became vice president of the country division of RCA Records, added something to the mood. He put violins and French horns into the sessions he produced in the 1960s, feeling that this would broaden the appeal of the records. The Nashville sound thus became an easy listening music that characterized country sessions and pop sessions alike.

Gradually the distinctions began to blur between country and pop, giving birth to a new "country pop" music. Atkins later thought that perhaps he had gone too far in broadening the appeal; he feared that country was losing its identity. Most fans were not bothered, however. Vastly different forms of country could coexist as far as they were concerned. They did not find it inconsistent to listen to and enjoy a hard country artist one minute and a country pop artist the next.

The growing popularity of country music on the radio showed that audiences liked the new country sound. At the start of the 1960s, not long after country's competitive war with rock music, there were about 75 stations programming country music full time. There were several hundred a few years later, and by the late 1970s there were more than 1,200.

Clearly, easy listening country and country pop had grown up naturally as part of country music. If Atkins had not taken the lead, someone else would have. Even before the advent of·the Nashville sound, one of the stars of the "Grand Ole Opry," the traditional country institution, was Jim Reeves, a singer with a smooth pop style. Reeves, who was killed in a plane crash in 1964, sang songs that told a story, but he had an easy listening style that made him known as the singer "with the velvet touch."

Many country performers were as ready for the new sound as the fans were. Glen Campbell was one of them. He was so successful as a country pop star that he had a highly rated weekly program on the CBS television network during the late 1960s. Songwriter John Loudermilk also welcomed the new sound in country music. He said that he had not forgotten his country roots—the

Modern-day Nashville

memory, for example, of "taking a bath in the kitchen while listening to country music from the radio on top of the ice box." People like Loudermilk have the sound of a banjo or fiddle in their backgrounds. But that doesn't mean that they have to be satisfied "with three chords and a bass and a steel." That is their heritage, "but we want to offer a whole lot more," said Loudermilk.

"Outlaw" Waylon Jennings

The 1970s: A New Image 7

For most of its commercial history, country music had been trying to shake the image of the "hick," the "hayseed," the "hillbilly." In the 1970s country succeeded, for the most part. Like anything else, the industry was subject to criticism, but few outside observers laughed anymore.

One of the last traces of the country stereotype lay in the highly successful syndicated television show "Hee Haw." That show, however, was an obvious caricature of the hillbilly image. It demonstrated that country people were secure enough to laugh at themselves, and to make money while they were laughing. The talent and professionalism found in country music simply could not be disrupted.

In the 1970s country music wore a new face. While the heritage and tradition had not been forgotten, there was practically no area of the industry that had not undergone some transformation.

For example, in the 1960s a country radio station may not have been able to thrive in metropolitan New York City. In the 1970s WHN Radio did. WHN adopted a country format in 1973 and, by 1977, had approximately 1,500,000 listeners and ranked second in its market in the 25-49 age group—a key group for advertisers.

Another difference between the new country music industry and the old was the existence of female as well as male singing stars. For 40 years women had rarely occupied an influential place in the industry. Even such famous pioneer performers as "Mother Maybelle" Carter and her cousin Sara were members of a group, not individual stars. The Carter Family was headed by A. P. Carter, Sara's husband. In 1936 Patsy Montana's record "I Want to be a Cowboy's Sweetheart" was the first record by a woman to sell more than one million copies. But Patsy wasn't a solo star, either. She performed with a group, the Prairie Ramblers, and with a radio program, the WLS "National Barn Dance."

The situation began to change gradually after World War II with the breakthrough of such singers as Rose Maddox, Molly O'Day, and Kitty Wells. Kitty, who was elected to the Country Music Hall of Fame in 1976, had a hit record in the 1950s, "It Wasn't God Who Made Honky-Tonk Angels." She composed and recorded it in angry response to a song released by Hank Thompson, "The Wild Side of Life," which maintained that women were created to be unfaithful to men. Kitty Wells was the first "queen of country music," but in her day there weren't many other women competing with her for the title.

Another popular female performer of the 50s was Patsy Cline, who won the Arthur Godfrey Talent Scout contest in 1957 with her rendition of "Walkin' after Midnight." Patsy seemed to have the potential of becoming a superstar, but her career was cut tragically short in 1963 when she was killed in a plane crash along with two other country musicians, Cowboy Copas and Hawkshaw Hawkins.

A close friend of Patsy's was Loretta Lynn, the "coal miner's daughter" from Butcher Hollow, Kentucky. (In her thick twang, Loretta still pronounces the name of her hometown Butcher "Holler.") Loretta became a star herself in the 1960s, was eventually recognized as the unofficial "queen" of the industry, and in 1972 became the first woman to be named "Entertainer of the Year" by the Country Music Association. By the 1970s other women, including Dolly Parton, Lynn Anderson, and Tammy Wynette, had attained superstar status.

The emergence of female singing stars was a factor in the expanding country market. Most buyers of country music records were (and still are) women, particularly married women between 35 and 49. They probably knew what Loretta Lynn and others were singing about when the message of the song concerned, for example, unfaithful men who drank too much.

The country industry also started cultivating the youth market in the 1970s. It got a younger image by making more recording opportunities available to artists like Johnny Rodriguez, who was born in 1952, and Tanya Tucker, born in 1958. Tanya had her first hit, "Delta Dawn," in 1971, when she was just 13 years old.

The "Grand Ole Opry" had its own new image. In 1974 it moved from the Ryman Auditorium, its home for more than 40 years, into a new $15-million Grand Ole Opry House, the largest radio and television broadcasting studio in the world. The Opry house became part of Opryland, U.S.A., a $31-million entertainment park featuring live music of various types. The expansion and improvement of the Opry facilities provided evidence of the continuing importance of Nashville in country music. Obviously, the city had retained its leadership in the industry; for instance, during the 1970s about 15,000 recording sessions were held there annually.

But country music meant more than just Nashville and the Opry, even though those were the most readily identifiable symbols of the industry.

Many of the most famous stars of the 1970s, such as Glen Campbell, Merle Haggard, and Johnny Cash, did not belong to the "Grand Ole Opry." They felt that they could do quite well without it, and, of course, they were right.

Some other performers were anti-Nashville or anti-establishment. Called "outlaws" or "renegades" of country music, they were constantly battling with executives in Music City, U. S. A., because they wanted more freedom to produce their own kind of music. Waylon Jennings, Willie Nelson, Kris Kristofferson, and Tompell Glaser were among the leaders of the outlaw (sometimes termed the "progressive") movement. Jennings, along with Linda Ronstadt, Emmylou Harris, and others, was instrumental in popularizing the new country rock sound of the 1970s. Nelson, a songwriter and honky-tonk singer who was once part of the Nashville establishment, moved back to his home state of Texas in 1970. He set up a headquarters in Austin that became a musical center for the progressive wing of country music.

California became another center of country music. Buck Owens and Merle Haggard produced music in Bakersfield (nicknamed "Buckersfield" or "Nashville West"), and numerous stars worked out of the Los Angeles area. In 1965 the Academy of Country and Western Music was founded in Los Angeles to promote country in western states, just as the Country Music Association promoted the industry throughout the entire nation. Evidently the "western" in the name caused some confusion about whether it referred to a region of the nation or to a style of music, so the name of the organization was changed to the Academy of Country Music.

Obviously, many changes took place in the 1970s, and not very quietly either. The country music industry was too big (making about $400 million annually) for everyone to agree about what it should be doing. Varying opinions on what was best for the artists, the writers, the record companies, and the public were unavoidable. Some people were upset over pop singers getting country music awards. Olivia Newton John was named "Best Female Vocalist" in 1974 by the Country Music Association, and John Denver got the "Entertainer of the Year" award in 1975. But crossovers were nothing new. If country music was the music of the public, then the public had to decide what country music was and who country music artists were (even if sometimes they were artists like John Denver).

In any event, the industry has always been able to satisfy its fans' appetites while furthering its own commercial welfare. Debates will continue about how the industry should conduct itself, and the country image will keep changing. Folks in country music will not forget their heritage, but, like John Loudermilk, they will "want to offer a whole lot more." The country performers of the future will not be afraid to add new sounds to the old.

Dolly Parton is one of today's female superstars of country music.

Index